For
PHILIP & JOAN HANES,

for doing more than anyone we know
to make North Carolina a place worth living in

BLUES &
ROOTS
RUE &
BLUETS

A Garland for the Appalachians

by
Jonathan Williams

Photographs by Nicholas Dean

Grossman Publishers, N.Y., 1971

Text Copyright © 1971 by Jonathan Williams
Photographs Copyright © 1971 by Nicholas Dean
All rights reserved
First published in 1971 by Grossman Publishers
44 West 56th Street, New York, N.Y. 10019
Published simultaneously in Canada by
Fitzhenry and Whiteside, Ltd.
SBN 670-17650-8
Library of Congress Catalogue Card Number: 76-156947
Printed in U.S.A.

Acknowledgments

Jonathan Williams would like to thank George Sadek and Joe Lucca of the Indiana University Design Program, and their students Ann Wilkinson and David Ahlsted, for their initial interest in a number of the concrete-poems in this collection. Thanks also to Doyle Moore and Arthur Korant, University of Illinois Fine Arts Department; Dan Haberman, *Graphic Arts Typographers*, New York City; Rose Slivka, *Craft Horizons* magazine, New York City; James Laughlin, *New Directions; The New York Times;* Richard Walser, *The North Carolina Miscellany* (1962); Emmett Williams, *The Something Else Press;* Stephen Bann, *London Magazine Editions;* Ian Hamilton Finlay, *The Wild Hawthorn Press*, Dunsyre, Lanarkshire, Scotland; Geof Hewitt, *Kumquat Press*, Montclair, New Jersey; William J. Brown, *Penland School of Crafts;* Persis Grayson, *Southern Highland Handicraft Guild;* and, finally, to Ronald Johnson for his abiding perspicacity . . . Charles Mingus, the Redoubtable, suggested "Blues & Roots" to me, and I hope he won't mind it being applied to the Big Foot Country . . . To the *Aspen Institute for Humanistic Studies* the poet's bounden appreciation for its support as a scholar-in-residence (1967-68). The opportunity to sit down and to use the Institute's facilities pulled the book together after five years of scatter.

Nicholas Dean would like to thank Gene Schwaab for his early interest and help in the project, and Polaroid Corporation, particularly the late Meroë Morse and Dr. Edwin H. Land for their patience and support. A number of these photographs were originally made as part of the documentation for the Department of the Interior, Federal Interdepartmental Task Force on the Potomac, and special thanks must go to the Honorable Stewart L. Udall, then Secretary of the Interior, and to George Hartzog, Director, National Park Service. Thanks also to the Society of Heliographers, *Heliography*, and to Clark Coolidge, *Joglars*. Over the seven years of photographing the Appalachians, a number of individuals have fed, housed, transported, and encouraged me. Thanks to all of them, and particularly to Grace Mayer, Nickie Wilson, Ansel Adams and Scott and Dottie Odell. Finally, none of this could have come about without my wife, Zibette, who put up with it all.

Introduction

BONJOUR, MONSIEUR COURBET!

Great title for a rambler's introduction to a mountain book that will seek to 'hesitate' its gentle readers. But, then, you would have to know the painting with that title. Assuming you are what George Corley Wallace says his neighbors in Barbour County, Alabama are—"*kindly, intelligent, educated, and refined*"—, we're sure you do know. However, if you honest-to-god don't, either go look at a book on Courbet or get ready to start calling me a Fascist Elitist Aristocrat or a Spoonbread Mafioso, because this is *my* book and you get what I want you to get.

"I, too, though I do not know what year it began, have long yielded to the wind like a loosened cloud and, unable to give up my wandering desires, have taken my way . . ." That is the Japanese diarist and poet, Basho, about to set off in 1689 on his famous *Narrow Road to the Deep North*. I, on the contrary, do know when it began for me, this thing of taking to shank's mare and doing without wheels. It was late May, 1961. Having spent $368.67 for Kelty packs, Mr. L. L. Bean's Maine Guide Shoes (and much else besides), and Eddie Bauer's sleeping bags, Ronald Johnson—the only poet in eastern America mad enough to come along—and I ate a huge breakfast at the Smith House in Dahlonega, Georgia and were driven to the southern terminus of the Appalachian Trail. From Springer Mountain we then spent the next 110 days inching up the spine of the range until we ran out of time and desire just at Bear Mountain Bridge on the Hudson. It was 1457 miles, give or take a few.

The medical virtues of such a piece of idiocy were quick to see, for I was already 32 and hadn't done anything more than engage in mythical softball games at Black Mountain College and bend my elbow for a decade: 35 pounds lost; pulse rate lowered by 8 counts per minute; blood pressure lowered to something ridiculous like 100/60. What took much longer to calculate was the effect of walking on my poems. From this almost four months away from High Culture, I finally sensed there was a lot *underfoot* in a literal way. It's not that I hadn't read Thoreau on how the inner-workings of a square yard of God's firmament could keep him happily occupied for years. And then there was Dr. Williams's poem where Chief One Horn is talking to the constipated prospector and he gashes a balsam and gathers the gum that oozes out in a tin spoon, which does just the trick. Moral being: "*You can do lots/if you know/what's around you/No bull.*" Peregrinating taught me the kind of localism I like best—the kind that's been everywhere else first. Which is the kind that allows Mae West to make such Delphic utterances as: use what's lying around the house and let it all hang out! Charles Ives, enraptured, fell for that one heavily.

So, for the past 10 years I have been walking, adding some thousands of miles to the long trek along the Appalachians; e.g., the Wye River from its confluence with the Severn below Chepstow, up the valley to the spring in the side of Great Plynlimon; the Pennine Way from Airedale to the Cheviot; the Lake District for two months; Snowdonia; Land's End, along the north coasts of Cornwall and Devon and Somerset to the Mendip Hills. And, always, trips in the Great Smokies, the Georgia Blue Ridge, the Nantahalas, the Pisgahs, the Unakas. My poetic 'method,' then, is *Peripatetic*, and such findings-out are inclined to be brief and quick—something between *epigram* and *epiphyte*, where you make it up out of the air, on the run . . . Consider this: three men are hiking the Appalachian Trail. The mycologist is the one who knows to look for oaks and apple trees on a north slope and, hence, for morels. The archaeologist won't have to stub his toe to spot the arrowhead or the pot shard. The poet is the one who wants to stop with the local boy who is digging ramps on the side of Big Bald Mountain and hear what kind of talk he has in his head.

Poets are forever seeing things, whether Angels in trees, or just things written on the sides of buses like JESUS SAVES & SATISFIES. ARE YOU? Poets are forever hearing things—"always the deathless music." I like to catch people speaking 'poems' who never heard of the word *poet*. It has been my business, along with many others my superiors (W. C. Williams, Louis Zukofsky, Lorine Niedecker, A. R. Ammons), to try to raise 'the common' to grace, to pay very close attention to the *earthy*, for one thing. Some people, accordingly (and even more refined than Governor Wallace's neighbors), find the poems vulgar. As my late friend Jack Wilcox used to assert: the poor world is horribly afflicted with people who couldn't say *shit* if they had a mouthful. I no more write for 'nice' people than I do for 'common' ones. I make poems for the people who want them. "He was southern, and he was a gentleman, but he was not a Southern Gentleman"—which is Allen Tate talking about Edgar-Allan-Poe-White-Trash. I sense my tradition there. My nature is mountainously suspicious, like the moonshiner's, of outside people who want to sample the wares. Clyfford Still says about his paintings: "I'd rather let my work burn than let certain people have it." Stravinsky is witty enough to realize that *Petrushka*, *The Firebird*, and *Le Sacre* have already had to survive a half-century of destructive popularity; whereas, the orchestral pieces of Schoenberg and Webern have been protected by 50 years of neglect. I don't want the Appalachians cluttered with senile, duck-billed Floridians. I want only readers who will meet me halfway in a poem—on their feet, not their fat. My 'America' is some few thousands of persons and a very few places in which I feel 'at home.' The rest is soap.

There is a lot of talk these days about the *Found Poem*. Criticasters would do well to remember the simple words of John Clare, Epping Forest, in 1848: "*I found the poems in the fields and only wrote them down.*" Frederick Sommer, a superb photographer and a superb intelligence, has told us: "What difference is there between what you find and what you make? You have to make it to find it. You have to find it to make it. You only find things you already have in your mind." PERIPATETIC: always on the go, always on the look-out. So-and-so has 'a way' with words. Better to say: a way, *of* words, made, un-made, in the going to and fro. In any event, we did not make the World, we just put a few words together, from here and there, from outside as well as inside. What did Goethe say?: *Das Wahre war schon laengst gefunden*—the Truth was found already long ago. (That is for groovy people who think nothing on earth happened, or mattered, before the birth of their 1968 Mustang.)

One section of texts is called "Countrified Concretions." I spent 10 years as a student of Charles Olson, who devoted his abundant energies to the demonstration that the life of poetry came *by ear*. One day Ian Hamilton Finlay, the Scots poet, smiled and quietly suggested to me that the contrary, *by eye*, was equally true. I have come to agree, and so you will find in the section some poems that have no noise in them at all, poems that do no public pleading or private screaming, poems that look back at you as mindlessly (almost) and coolly as nature's signs. Nature, according to a friend who is a crystallographer, has some 217 ways of putting together its structures. The concrete mode in poetry is only 'one way,' with its particular uses and particular pitfalls. Lyric poets tend to lose their speed as they age, like fireballers in the Majors. I am prepared to throw *anything* I can at the gentle reader: fork-ball, slider, palm-ball, spitter, knuckler—he's not going to get an inside edge on me if I can help it. Also, it keeps him awake at the plate . . . I recall an evening at Chapel Hill, A scholiast, with very eccentric notions on the *Cantos* of Ezra Pound, suddenly snarled: "Concrete poetry is nothing but masturbation!" Lordy, what is the poor visting poet to answer in public to that? What I had not the wit to reply was: "You do it your way, I'll do it mine." If you will simply look the concrete poems in the face and see that they are not plastic epics in disguise or lyrics in drag, then we'll both breathe easier. It is very easy to look at the poems in this book because Dana Atchley is one of the best typographers around. We have argued and peered, and argued some more, and finally been flabbergasted by some of the things that were found in the words as their visualization took place.

Finally, some thoughts on the photographs. Nicholas Dean has been tramping the Appalachians as long as I have, loaded with Rolleis, Mamiyaflexes, view-cameras, and all the gear. The New England end of the Trail is his province, but we have hiked the southern mountains together on occasion— once from Roan Mountain 150 miles southwest to Mt. Le Conte in the Smokies, during the fine April of 1968. We hope that you will find—in both words and images—a range and character that only years of familiarity and wandering could have produced. (This to me was the disappointment inherent in the book, *Appalachian Wilderness*, produced in 1970 by an excellent New Mexico photographer and an excellent New Mexico novelist—too much the feeling of buzzing in for the weekend to handle an 'assignment.') I never forget that the Reverend A. Rufus Morgan, of Franklin, North Carolina, has hiked up Le Conte over 100 times. Even though he is almost blind with age, he 'sees' new things each time. No man can ever know a mountain well enough.

Another thing about the Dean photographs. They, like the poems, have no truck with the prettification of nature that is one of the curses of Nature-Loving and of Nature, Inc. organizations. Imogen Cunningham puts it very well: ". . . one must not have a too-pronounced notion of what constitutes beauty in the external, and above all not worship it.

To worship beauty for its own sake is narrow and one surely cannot derive from it that aesthetic pleasure which comes from finding beauty in the commonest things." Again, we have made a book *al que quiere*. Many will prefer Grace Hazard Conkling and Jesse Stuart. I don't know that there's an answer to that, except watch out where you step! (There *is* an answer: read books by William Bartram, Horace Kephart, Allen Eaton, and Harry Caudill.)

Meantime, let's have a little party on the porch, with Earl Scruggs doing the pickin' and Johnny Niles doing the singin'. The first snort of vintage popskull from over on Spill Corn Creek will be in honor of William Bartram, for finding *Franklinia Alatamaha;* the second, in honor of André Michaux, for finding *Shortia Galicifolia;* the third, for Charles Ives, for *Bringing Everything Back Alive.* And the fourth is to put a Garland on this range we call *Appalachian* since Cabeza de Vaca heard the word in 1528. Whether the rattlesnake and the pileated woodpecker have a name for it doesn't matter. It is more theirs than ours.

Highlands, North Carolina
January 27, 1971

Postscriptum: A young colleague, having read the foregoing, remarks: "Gosh all hemlock, Masked Rider, you sure have funny feelings about readers—now you want them, now you don't. One minute you say poems are only for those who want them. Ok. But the next you are seized with Procrustean Paranoia and start trying to cut them down to size. *Up-tight*, I'd say." Well, says I, maybe so . . . I remember a dream in which I started a World Series game, and there was nobody in the stands . . . It's not that I want to strike everybody out with the fast stuff. I just want them to learn to hit the poem where it's pitched—that's BINGO, that's good for both sides. Of course, the baseball metaphor only pushes so far, but it's used to suggest a Louis Sullivan insight: "A pine tree is *not* an oak tree." Spare us those readers who watch, frozen, only for *their* particular pitch. In the immortal words of Early Wynn: "If she tried to dig in too much on me, I'd brushback my own grandmother." Young colleague remarks: "Well, I'm glad your poems are made out of words, not ideas."

*Common
Words in
Uncommon
Orders*

Bea Hensley Hammers an Iron Chinquapin Leaf
On His Anvil Near Spruce Pine
& Cogitates on the Nature of Two Beauty Spots

in the Linville Gorge I
know this place

now it's a rock wall
you look up
it's covered in punktatum all
the way to Heaven

that's a
sight

●

up on Smoky
you ease up at daybust
and see the first
light in the tops of the tulip trees

now boys that just naturally
grinds and polishes
the soul

makes it
normal
again

I mean it's really
pretty!

Daddy Bostain, the Moses of the Wing Community Moonshiners,
Laments from His Deathbed the Spiritual Estate
Of One of His Soul-Saving Neighbors:

God bless her pore
little ol
dried up
soul!

jest make
good kindlin wood
fer Hell...

some folks say
the injuns made 'em
like lie-detectors
called 'em
hoo-doo sticks

feller
in Salisbury, Noth Caylini
made the first
whimmy-diddle I seen

I whittle seven
kind: thisuns king
size, thisuns jumbo, thisuns
extry large

here's a single, here's one
double, here's a triple and why right here
here's a forked 'un

been whittlin' whimmy-diddles come
ten year, I reckon you'd
care to see my other toys,
boys, I got some fine
flippers-dingers, fly-
killers and bull-roarers, I can

kill a big fly at 60 feet

watch here

The Hermit Cackleberry Brown, on Human Vanity:

caint call your name
but your face is easy

come sit

now some folks figure theyre
bettern
cowflop they
aint

not a bit

just good to hold the world together
like hooved up ground

thats what

Lee Ogle Ties a Broom & Ponders Cures for Arthuritis

lands them fingers really
dreadfulled me I
couldnt tie
nary broom one

had to soak em in water
hot as birds blood

then I heared this ol man from Kentucky say
take a jug of apple juice just juice not cider
pour the epsum salts to it and
take as much as you kin

bein fleshy I kin take
right smart but
boys you know it moves a mans bowels
somethin terrible

well boys it just
naturally killed that arthuritis
lost me some weight too
and I
still tie thesehere brooms

pretty good

The September Satisfaction of Uncle Iv Owens:

I got
a rat-proof
crib!

Snuffy Smith's Colossal Maw From War-Woman Dell

more mouth on
that woman

than ass
on a goose

The Nostrums of the Black Mountain Publican

best thing
for roomatiz,
Homer, is

a great big ol messa
Woolly-Booger

if God
made anything better
he kep it
for Hissef

but boys lemme
tell you:

DON'T EAT NO
HAIRPIE
ON FRIDAY!

Logger to Dozer

if you work
for me,
son,
you got to
shit
and go
get
it

The Custodian of a Field of Whisky Bushes
By the Nolichucky River Speaks:

took me a pecka real ripe tomaters up
into the Grassy Gap
one night

and two quarts of good stockade
and just laid there

sippin and tastin and lookin agin the moon
at them sorta fish eyes in the jar
you get when its right

boys Im talkin bout somethin
good

A Ride in a Blue Chevy From Alum Cave Trail to Newfound Gap

goin' hikin'?
git in!

o the Smokies are ok but me
I go for Theosophy,
higher things, Hindu-type philosophy,
none of this licker and sex, I
like it
on what we call the astral plane,
I reckon I get more i-thridral
by the hour

buddy, you won't believe this but
how old you reckon the earth is?
the earth is
precisely 156 trillion years old—
I got this book from headquarters in
Wheaton, Illinois
says it is!

I'll tell you somethin' else:
there are exactly 144 kinds of people on earth—
12 signs and the signs change
every two hours,
that's 144, I'm Scorpio,
with Mars over the water

here's somethin' else innerestin':
back 18 million years
people was only one sex, one sex only ...
I'd like to explain that,
it's right here in this pamphlet,
50 cents ...

never married, lived with my mother in Ohio,
she died, I'm over in Oak Ridge
in a machine shop, say,
what kind of place
is Denver?
think I'll sell this car, go to Denver,
set up a Center ...

name's Davis,
what's yours?

Cracker-Barrel Reveries on the Tune "Pax Americana"

"Us common people run this country!" George Wallace

feller over in
franklin
says hes got thishere book
says that fbi feller hoover
says that nigger preacher kings
nothin
but a tarnation communist

and i reckon you boys
heared on the tv this
walter jenkins hes
some kind of unnatchrul sex prevert why
you know them seven chillun
must be lightbulbs
you just now it

just like you know ol castro
and them jew boys in new york
got us into veetnam

some things bes plain obvious

why the barber feller was sayin
just yesterday
he said put the bombs to em boys drop em
all over them russkis and
the dadblame chinamens too and
might as well drop em on ol dee gawl
too hes got the big mouth dont he

i mean put it to em all
i mean buddy we could stop all this foolishness up north

why some things bes plain obvious

people get
what they want

once we all grew shellot
potato onions everybody
around here have run out of
seed E. E. Seaton
of Jonesboro
Tennessee done heard
about this

•

the Fourth-a-July
Holiday
passed off in this part
very quiet

•

that snake were such
peculiar looking
to me I'm afraid I
couldn't give it justice
trying to describing it but it
didn't act mean like
it tryed to be
pretty like
it did

Aunt Creasy, on Work:

shucks
I make the livin

uncle
just makes the livin
worthwhile

The Ancient of Days

would that I
had known Aunt Cumi
Woody

C-u-m-i, pronounced
Q-my

she lived in the Deyton Bend Section of Mitchell
County, North Carolina many years ago

there is one of Bayard Wootten's photographs of her
standing there with her store-bought
teeth, holding a coverlet

she sheared her sheep, spun
and dyed her yarn in vegetable dyes,
and wove the coverlet

in indigo, the brown from walnut roots,
red from madder, green from hickory ooze, first,
then into the indigo (the blue pot)

Cumi, from the Bible
(St. Mark 5:41)

Talitha Cumi:
"Damsel, I say unto thee, arise!"

she is gone, she
enjoyed her days

Granny Donaldson Scoffs at Skeptics & the Uninitiated
As She Works up a Cow-Blanket
(Of Homespun, Crocheting & Appliqué)
Up a Branch Near Brasstown, Georgia

Question: whut fer
              thesehyar
              animules
              be,
              Granny?

Answer: haint fer
              to name! why Adam's
              Off-Ox
              in thishyar
              Garden
              haint got
              no name
              neither
              yet

              but the Lord's
              liable to call
              thishyar
              tree
              Arber
              Vity

              hit's got
              thishyar
              sarpint
              in it

Aunt Dory Ellis, of Penland, Remembers
When She Fell in Her Garden at the Home Place
And Broke Her Hip in 19 and 56

the sky was high,
white clouds passing
by, I lay
a hour in that petunia patch

hollered,
and knew I was out of whack

Mrs. Sadie Grindstaff, Weaver & Factotum,
Explains the Work-Principle to the Modern World

I figured
anything anybody
could do a lot of I
could do a little
of

mebby

Uncle Iv Surveys His Domain From His Rocker of a Sunday Afternoon
As Aunt Dory Starts to Chop Kindling

Mister Williams
lets youn me move
tother side the house

the woman
choppin woods
mite nigh the awkerdist thing
I seen

Tom Merton's Neighbor, Andy Boone, Looks Up:

Father,

when the wild turkeys
fly south
and say

W

A

R

with their wings,

it's liable to be
war

Three Sayings From Highlands, North Carolina:

but pretty though as
roses is
you can put up with
the thorns

Doris Talley, Housewife & Gardener

you live until you die—
if the limb don't fall

Butler Jenkins, Caretaker

your points is blue
and your timing's
a week off

Sam Creswell, Auto Mechanic

From Uncle Jake Carpenter's
Anthology of Death on Three-Mile Creek

Loney Ollis
age 84
dide jun 10 1871

grates dere honter
wreked bee trees for hony
cild ratell snak by 100
cild dere by thousen

i nod him well

The Epitaph on Uncle Nick Grindstaff's Grave
On the Iron Mountain Above Shady Valley, Tennessee:

LIVED ALONE

SUFFERED ALONE

DIED ALONE

A
Week from the
Big Pigeon
To the Little
Tennessee River

Davenport Gap

the tulip poplar is not a
poplar it is a magnolia:
liriodendron tulipifera

the young grove on the eastern slopes of
Mt. Cammerer reminds me
of the two huge trees
at Monticello, favorites
of Mr. Jefferson;

and of the Virginia lady
quoting Mr. Kennedy:

the recent gathering of
Nobel Prize Winners at the
White House—the most
brilliant assemblage
in the dining room
since Mr. Jefferson
dined there

alone . . .

a liriodendron
wind, a liriodendron
mind

DeWitt Clinton (besides
looking like Lon
Chaney on tobacco-tax stamps)
comes to the eye
in *clintonia borealis*—

of which fair green lily
there are millions
on this mountain

it is a mantle
for fire-cherry, yellow birch,
and silver bell

Tri-Corner Knob

here the shelter's
in a stand of
red spruce and balsam fir

for dinner: lamb's-quarters,
cress from the streams
on Mt. Guyot,
wood sorrel, and
cold argentine beef, chased with
tangerine kool-aid

False Gap

no *Schwarzwald* stuff,
keine Waldeinsamkeit,

no magic grouse, no
Brothers Grimm—just
Canadian hemlock, mossed and lichened,
like unto maybe
Tertiary time . . .

too much for a haiku?
you hike it and see

Ice Water Springs

no,

it's not like the woods
on the Rockefeller Estate
at Tarrytown

it's not
like the woods on
the Biloxi River

it's not like
the woods in the State of
Tabasco

no, it
isn't

LeConte High-Top

under the rondelay
the sun

into the wind and rain a
winter wren

again, again—

its song
needling the pines

Silers Bald

just in front of the
round iron john
in the beech grove

the fresh bear droppings
give you

something
to think about

Russell Fields

over Thunderhead
in meadows of
Turk's-cap lilies, white hellebore,
saxiphrage and St. John's wort...

looking into Cades Cove,
that visionary cup
of silent fields,
220 campsites
pepsi-cola machines

and even
a Park Service sign
pointing up a hill
saying

FALLOUT SHELTER

Countrified
Concretions

Lipstick Sign Under the Concrete Bridge Over Middle Creek

A3 TALK BACK TREMBLING LIPS

33⅓ Norma Jean STEREO

A4 LET'S GO ALL THE WAY

C3 WILD! WILD! WILD!

33⅓ Stonewall Jackson STEREO

C4 GIVE IT BACK TO THE INDIANS

E7 MR & MRS USED TO BE

33⅓ Ernest Tubbs STEREO

E8 DERN YA

G5 TRUCK DRIVER'S QUEEN

33⅓ Johnny Cash STEREO

G6 THE GREAT PRETENDER

H1 RE-INCARNATION

33⅓ The Beach Boys STEREO

H2 CHUG-A-LUG

K5 MOTHER-IN-LAW

33⅓ Dale and Grace STEREO

K6 DANG ME

Wurlitzer Top Tunes*
(Select Stereo Program by Famous Artists)
Press Golden Bar, Insert Coin,
"Musical Fun For Everyone!"

Applewhite Max
Bell Corydon
Chiltoshey Going Back Mrs
Cody Verlous
Cope Ode
Cox Plato
Crisp Gentry
Dalton Dock
Evitt Delphia Mrs
Flack Kolin
Foxx Zollie Rev
Game Gertrude
Gibson Pink
Good Colon L Rev
Gribble Geneva
Huggins Rass
Imperato Pat
Jones Vestal
Johnson John Bunion
King Hill
Keener Maiden
Kiser Julian (Bug)
Keen Yeoman
Love Jeter
Mashburn Angeline
Muse O.U.

Moss Floda
Norton Paschal
Orr Deaver
Owl Frell
Painter Fern
Peek Benlon
Polk James K.
Pickens Excellent Fine
Picklesimer Turley
Queen Kennith
Quiet Lily
Rogers Gas Island
Rainwater Veezey
Strong Hope
Sneed Cam
Shook Troy
Tweed Strang
Undergrowth Homer
Van Lyon
Webb Zero
Wold Maude
Womack Kibby
Whittle Chester
Ward Milas
Wood Cooter
Youngbird Rufus

Selected Listings from the Western Carolina Telephone Company's
Directory (Bryson City, Cashiers, Cherokee-Whittier, Cullowhee,
Franklin, Highlands, Sylva)

you could hear an ant
fart
it was that
quiet

Aubade

What Are the Names of the
More Remote Mountains of Northwestern Georgia?
Horn
John

Lavender

Turkey

eleg

Dug Down

Little Sand

Dirtseller

The Remains of a Sign, Mitchell County, North Carolina

of the thickness / of the Small / of a lusty Man's Leg

Ye Rattle-Snake

The Traditionally Accommodating Spirit of the Mountains
Shows Up in Neon in Franklin, NC, Once Nikwasi, a Cherokee Capital.

Rusticated Variations on a Poem by Ladislav Novak

A Mnemonic Wallpaper Pattern for Southern Two-Seaters

bulldogs
stamp out
dragon fire

PEACHES HEAR

---

pleeze
vot fer lindin

3 Graffiti, in the Vicinity of
The Mikado Baptist Church,
Somewhere Deep in a Poverty-Pocket

BUSTHAID
BLOCKADE
POPSKULL

What Are the Names
Of the Three Tutelary Hamadryads
Of the Hickory Grove
On Dirty John Creek in the Nantahalas?

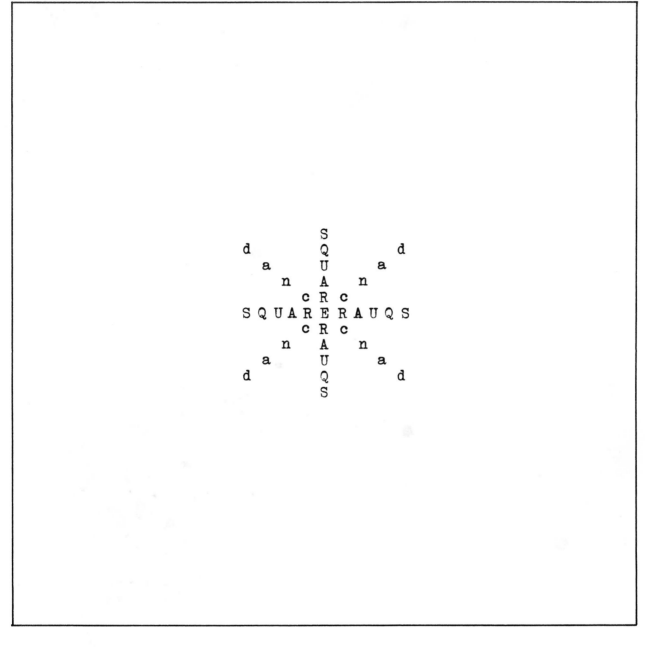

Do That Jawja Rang-Tang!

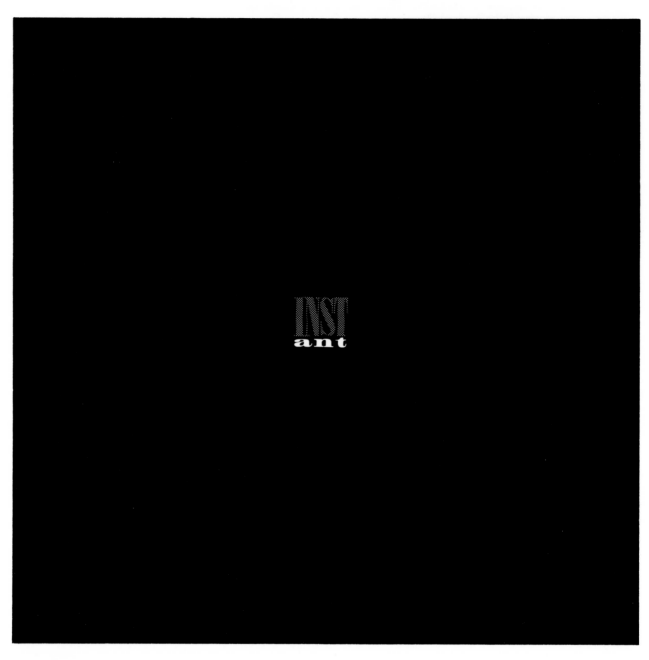

While Down at the Formicary, Time Flies

```
                                                                   lb
Angelica Root...............................     .35
Balm Gilead Buds (dry)......................     .45
Beeswax, Yellow.............................     .20
Birch Bark (thick, rossed)..................     .01
Black Cohosh Root (bone dry)................     .07
Blood Root..................................     .23
Boneset, Leaves and Tops (no stems).........     .08
Cramp Bark (genuine)........................     .35
Echinacea Root..............................     .50
Ginseng Root, Wild Southern.................   12.00
Ginseng, Cultivated.........................    2.50
Golden Seal Root............................    2.00
Indian Hemp Root, Black.....................     .10
Jimson Leaves (dry and bright)..............     .06
Lady Slipper Root...........................    1.25
Liverwort Leaves............................     .15
May Apple Root (Mandrake Root)..............     .30
Pleurisy Root (Butterfly Root)..............     .20
Queen of the Meadow Root....................     .02
Samson Snake Root...........................     .75
Sassafras Bark of Root (rossed).............     .35
Senega Snake Root...........................     .75
Serpentaria (Virginia Snake Root)...........    2.00
Star Grass Root.............................     .80
Strawberry Leaves...........................     .10
Tansy Leaves................................     .25
Texas Snake Root............................    2.00
Wahoo Bark of Root..........................    1.25
Wild Cherry Bark (thin, young, rossed)......     .08
Wild Indigo Root (dry)......................     .05
Wild Ginger Root............................     .30
Wintergreen Leaves (bright).................     .35
Witch Hazel Leaves (bright).................     .12
Yarrow Herb.................................     .06
```

Items from a Collectors' Cash Price List
(Berries Roots Ginseng Herbs Beeswax Barks Flowers Leaves)
S. B. Penick & Co., Asheville, North Carolina
(The World's Largest Botanical Drug House)
"Everything We Buy Must Be Dry"

A Blazon, Built
Of the Commonest of All Common Eurasian Weeds
Of the Fields and the Wayside

WAHUHU WAHUHU WAH
UKU UGUKU UGUKU UGU
U HUHU HUHU HUHU HU
LU LALU LALU LALU LA
TU TALATU TALATU TAL
LILI TSIKI LILI TSIKI LILI
IKIKI TSIKIKI TSIKIKI T
U KAGU KAGU KAGU KA
WAYA WAYA WAYA WAYA
YEAH YEAH YEAH YEAH
NA GUNA GUNA GUNA GU
SASA SASA SASA SASAS
UNU KUNUNU KUNUNU
DUSTU DUSTU DUSTU D

A Chorale* of Cherokee Night Music
As Heard Through an Open Window in Summer Long Ago

*screech owl / hoot owl / yellow-breasted chat / jar-fly / cricket / carolina chickadee /
katydid / crow / wolf / beetle / turkey / goose / bullfrog / spring frog

Three Bears of Different Sizes,
Dreaming from Three Hollow Logs
on Mt. Kephart in the Great Smokies
on a Warm Day in February

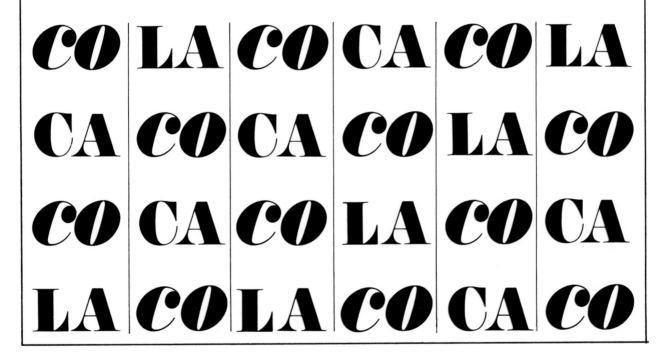

The Six-Pak (A Soda-Pop Sodality)

Red-Bone Heaven

KUK

KUK KUK

KUK·KUK

KUKKUK

A Pileated Woodpecker's Response to Four Dogwood Berries

U NEED JESUS GOOD BUDDY

Stone Sign
By the Bethel Temple Congregational Community Church's
Resident Theologaster
On the Banks of the Tallulah River

EULA'S
BAT
EUY
SHOPPE

Coming into Loafers Glory in The Valley of the Roan

Favorite Sun Candidate

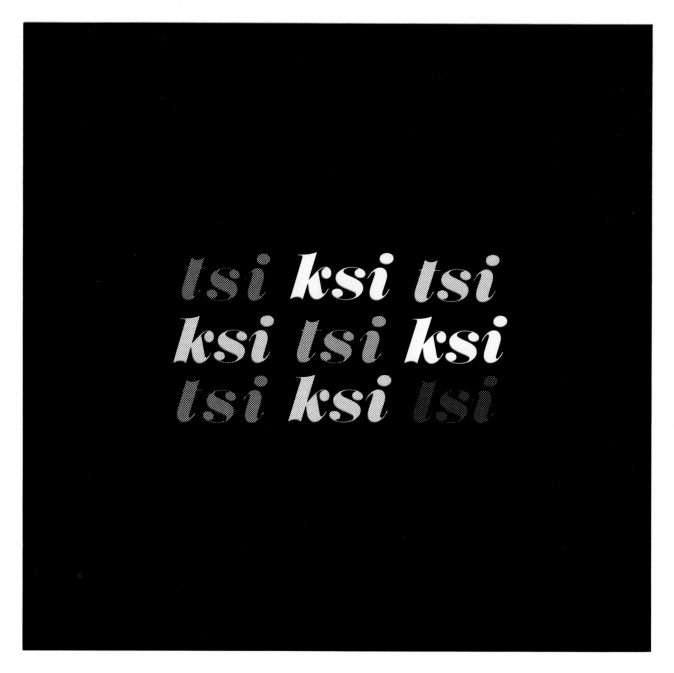

3 Ripples in the Tuckasegee River

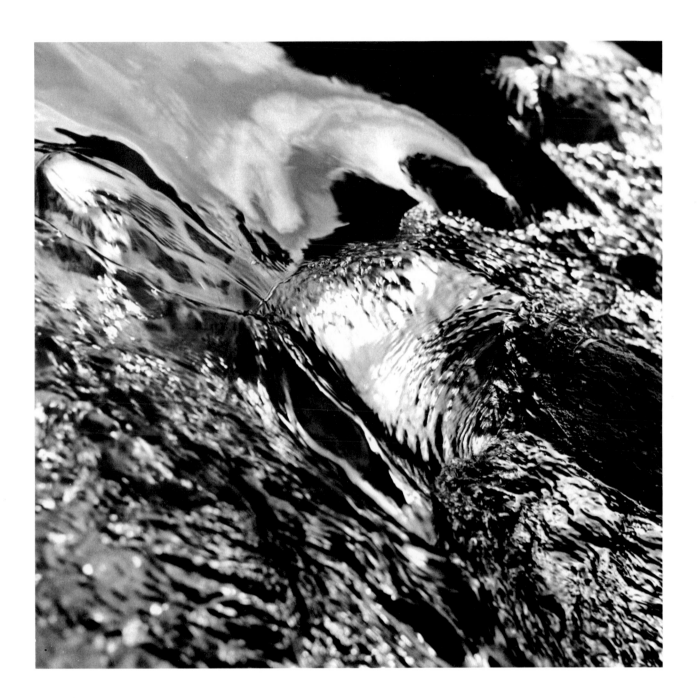

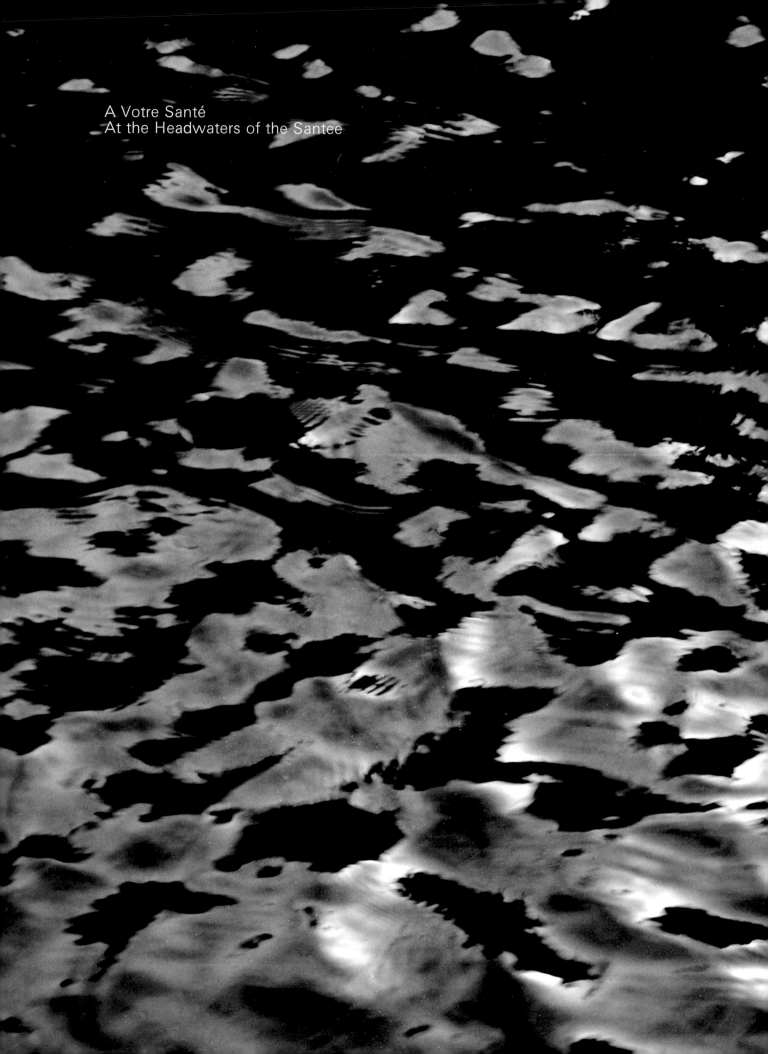

A Votre Santé
At the Headwaters of the Santee

"which water we drank of, it
coloring the excrements of Travelers,
by its Chalybid Quality,
as black as a Coal"

John Lawson

The Yellow Peril at Moore's Grocery

O'NAN'S AUTO SERVICE

John Chapman pulls off the highway towards Kentucky and casts a cold eye on the most astonishing sign in recent American letters.

ROX
FUR
SAL

A Sign Maker Between Possum Trot and Rabbit Hop
Entertains Us With a Triple Joycean Pun*

*cattle would lick the natural outcroppings of salt rock
 which would, among other things, lend gloss to their coats

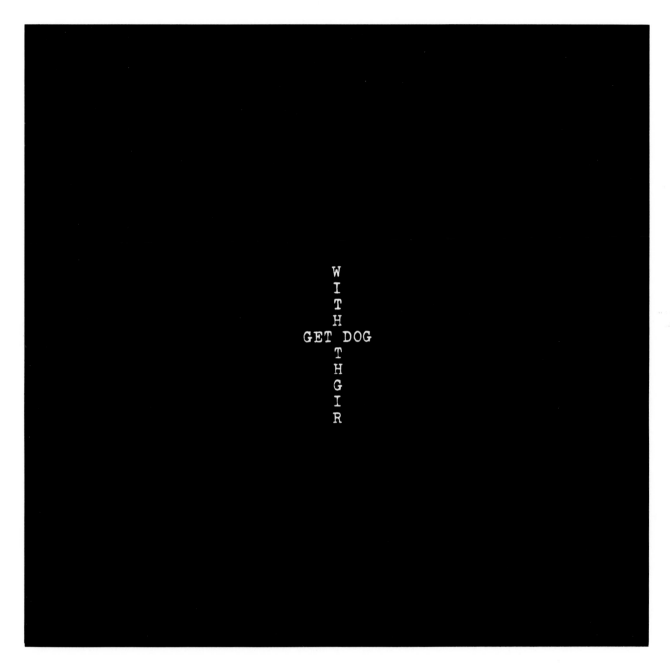

The World-Navel near Dahlonega, Jawja

BEPREPA REDTO MEETGO D

Paint Sign on a Rough Rock, Yonside of Boone Side of Shady Valley

Windfalls

a flame azalea, mayapple, maple, thornapple
plantation

a white cloud in the eye
of a white horse

a field of bluets moving
below the black suit
of William Bartram

bluets, or "Quaker Ladies," or some say
"Innocence"

bluets and the blue of gentians and
Philadelphia blue laws!

high hills,

stone cold
sober

as October

Cobwebbery

the best spiders for soup
are the ones under
stones—

ask the man who is one:
plain white american

(not blue gentian red indian yellow sun black carribean)

hard heart, cold
mind's found

a home
in the ground

"a rolling stone, *nolens volens,*
ladles no soup"

maw, rip them boards off
the side the house

and put the soup pot on

and plant us some petunias
in the carcass of the Chevrolet

and let's stay here
and rot in the fields

and sit still

Night Landscape in Nelson County, Kentucky

ah, Moon, shine
thou as amber in thy
charred-keg, hickory sky...

still as a still, steep
as a horse's face

3 Thefts from John Ehle's Prose

every night
the possums climb higher
in the persimmon trees

●

a red pumpkin
in a row of yellow pumpkins
in a field

●

better'n
a creek
fulla syrup

A Round of Nouns in Jackson County

Rough Butt Creek
to
Bearwallow Fork
to
Snaggy Bald
to
Mayapple Gap
to
Fern Mountain
to
Soapstone Gap
to
Rocky Face Cliff
to
Alum Knob
to
John Brown Branch
to
Hornyhead Mountain
to
Niggerskull Mountain
to
Sugar Creek Gap
to
Rough Butt Creek

Napolean Crossing the Rocky Mountains,
Sunrise on the Walls of Troy;

Tennessee Trouble in North Carolina,
Big Works of Tennessee;

Snail Trail,
Double Muscadine Hulls;

Catch Me If You Can!

The Action During the Pour-Down* at Plumorchard Gap Shelter,
September 29, 1964:

6:15 a.m.
one Samson's Snakeroot in a clump of Galax
at the spring

10:23 a.m.
sluggish black salamander grabs bristling cricket
by left hind leg
but   lets   go

12:50 p.m.
fresh deer droppings on the Trail
full of orange persimmon seeds

2:47 p.m.
a ripe persimmon plops on the ground
among the dogwoods

4:20 p.m.
one pink plastic rat-tail comb
washed clean in the fireplace

5:06 p.m.
a red spider rides, a yellow maple leaf
glides to earth

8:31 p.m.
flashlight batteries fade out
reading Joseph Mitchell's profile
of Little Joe Gould

*at Rosman, on the North Fork of the French Broad River
below the Balsam Mountains, the rain is reportedly 16 inches
in less than 24 hours.

Jeff Brooks, Wagon-Master of Andrews,
En Route to Franklin Through the Nantahalas:

no
other
sound

except

the creak
of leather

cave, it means cave

CHOLUK   (Choctaw jargon per Mobilian Trade Language,
                   Gulf Coast and Southeast, 1539 and pre-)

CHALAQUE (Portuguese, Gent. of Elvas' De Soto Chronicle,
                   1557)

CHERAQUI (French, Penicaut, 1699, in contact with Lower
                   Dialect, where *l* becomes *r*)

CHEROKEE (Eng. Gov. Johnson, 1708, probable ancestor of
                   P. Johnson, Gov. of Miss., still talking
                   Choctaw jargon)

the Cherokee form is *Tsalagi*, and means nothing;
they call themselves *Yunwiya*,
the principal people

A Note* on the European Background of
Sempervivum Tectorum, Which We Now Call
'Houseleek' or 'Hen-and-Chickens'

this wort,
which is named *prick madame,*
is produced on walls, and in stony places,
and on downs,
and on old barrows,

and from one root
it sendeth forth many minute boughs,
and they be full of leaves,
minute and long,
and sharp and fat,
and well oozy,
or *succulent,*

and the root of this wort
is without use!

*from the Rev. Thomas Oswald Cockayne's
LEECHDOMS, WORTCUNNING & STARCRAFT OF EARLY EANGLAND

The Leaf of Galax and the Habit of Pyrola

Iwauchuwa in Japan; *Shortia galicifolia* in Transylvania and Oconee counties in the southern Appalachians—the most legendary of our plants. Donald Culross Peattie is the custodian of the whole story. He has told it so beautifully in *Green Laurels* and in *The Great Smokies and the Blue Ridge* that it would be of no point for me to elaborate on his work. Suffice it, that a brief entry, dated December 8, 1788, in the journal of André Michaux was the beginning of a hundred years of investigation and search by Asa Gray, Charles Sprague Sargent, and other conspicuous American botanists. Michaux simply noted: ". . . I came across a new bush (*arbuste*) with notched leaves that was rampant on the mountainside not far from the river." He was at the headwaters of the Keowee (Kiwi, as he wrote it), below the confluence of the Horsepasture and Toxaway rivers as they have dropped from the ridge of the Balsam Mountains and levelled off above the present settlements of Tamassee and Jocassee in Oconee County, South Carolina. Today it is not difficult to find colonies of the plant under kalmia and rhododendron along the river.

There is another colony of plants further downriver these days, after the Keowee becomes the Savannah, there at Aiken/Augusta, where Thermonuclear Pale-Face works at the instruments of his destruction—or his salvation, it is probably one and the same. It seems questionable which species will outlast the other? The new flower-power dam put up by Duke Power tilts the balance in favor of man, but the America of Michaux and Bartram has been going down a rathole for a long time. It is interesting that William Bartram's grave is now unknown, though a two-day search in the Philadelphia area turned up for me the remains of father John. The stone is in the Quaker graveyard in Upper Darby, Pennsylvania, and the inscription reads: Approximate Grave of John Bartram . . .

If you despise a place long enough—this unruly continent, for instance—your own nature becomes somehow despicable. Man is a symbiot. There are places in the bald meadows of the Smokies where the bluets are windy clouds and the eye that reflects them is uncommonly lovely. Nowhere along the Appalachian Trail could I find a sacred grove, even in the Pennsylvania forest that Gifford Pinchot named for André and Francois Michaux. The trees were there, yet I could not find the citizens. Sacred for whom? to whom? The flawless boles of tulip poplars can be measured variously. Board feet by the hundred provide no wonder. I wondered whether the name of the god had not been drowned in the song of the wood thrush?

Paul McCartney's song "The Fool on the Hill" puts our deprivation as poignantly as I have heard it put. This magnificent composition, no less than the best of Schubert, Mahler, or Weill, atones for a lot in a deprived landscape, as does a visit to Michaux's handsome little plant—before it is covered by venal water.

Edward Dahlberg writes in *The Sorrows of Priapus:* "The difference between a civilized and a detestable nation is in its votive fruits, spices, and animals. The Philistines, to appease the God of Israel, returned the stolen Ark with golden replicas of hemorrhoids. Aaron had an oracular Rod upon which almonds budded, and Perseus named the city of Mycene after a woody mushroom. Lucretius mentions the majoram young suitors smeared on the doorposts of damsels. Solomon sang of the myrrh and sloes on the locks of the bridal door; Jesus ached for the alabaster of fragrant ointment the Pharisee denied him. 'Would to God that all the Lord's People were Prophets,' said Moses who sighed for men whose souls smelled of frankincense and orchard fruits."

Dr. Charles Wilkins Short, the doctor-botanist of Kentucky, for whom Asa Gray named the plant, must have been such.

La Source

the Conasauga and the
Coosawattee
make the

Oostanaula

the Oostanaula and the
Etowah
make the
Coosa

flow
so

Mr. Rufus Cook
Blairsville, Georgia

Dear Mr. Cook,

The past few weeks I have been attempting to locate some Indian rock carvings which my reading tells me are in Union County. These carvings do not seem to be those at Track Rock Gap. I have been there three or four times and the position and surroundings do not agree with what is in the books. When I talked to some men working on the new highway up to Jack's Gap, one of them said you would know if anybody did. So said the look-out ranger up on Brasstown Bald. I am interested because I am a writer and photographer, and because the Southern Highlands is the part of the world I like best. I've hiked the Appalachian Trail from Georgia to New Hampshire, and I've been exploring around Highlands since 1941, so, I know a little—but not nearly enough.

The first reference I encountered was a paper, "On the Pictographs of the North American Indians," by Garrick Mallery. This is contained in the *Fourth Annual Report of the Bureau of Ethnology*, published in Washington, DC in 1886. On page 23 it says this:

"Dr. M. F. Stephenson mentions, in *Geology and Mineralogy of Georgia* (Atlanta, 1871, page 199), sculptures of human feet, various animals, bear tracks, etc., in Enchanted Mountain, Union County, Georgia. The whole number of etchings is reported as one hundred and forty-six."

The only other mention is of an incised boulder in Forsyth County, Georgia, first noted by Charles C. Jones, Jr., in *Antiquities of the Southern Indians, etc.* (New York, 1873, page 377) . . . It seems a little odd that there is no mention of Track Rock.

Next I came across a legend of Enchanted Mountain in *Georgia's Landmarks, Memorials, and Legends* (Atlanta, 1913, 2 volumes, pages 457-60 in volume two), by Lucian Lamar Knight. This work strikes me as much less reliable than the Government publication mentioned initially above. However, it has a much fuller description. Mr. Knight indicates that his information comes from an old scrap-book belonging to a Dr. Stevenson, of Dahlonega. (The name leads me to wonder whether or not Dr. Stevenson is not the Dr. M. F. Stephenson of the first reference?)

Let me quote parts of this account, and see what you make of it:

"Ten miles north of the Blue Ridge Chain, of which it forms a spur, is the Enchanted Mountain, so called from the great number of tracks and impressions of the feet and hands of various animals to be found in the rocks . . . The number of well-defined tracks is one hundred and thirty-six, some of them quite natural and perfect, others rather rude imitations, and all of them, from the effects of time, have become more or less obliterated."

He notes 26 impressions of human feet. "A finely-turned hand, rather delicate, may be traced in the rocks near the foot of the great warrior." He mentions horse tracks, turkeys, turtles, terrapins, a bear's paw, a snake, and two deer.

As to the location he says: "On the morning of the 3rd of September, 1834, our party left the Nacoochee Valley . . . At six o'clock we arrived at the summit of the mountain . . . We advanced to the foot of the rock and spread out our breakfast on the 'table of stone' . . . Around us were piled huge heaps of loose rock . . . The rock upon which these impressions were found is an imperfect sort of soapstone . . . After excessive fatigue and no little danger, we were now ready to return home, but before descending the long slope we paused to feast our enraptured eyes upon one of the most magnificent panoramas to be found on the North American continent . . . On the east is Tray, peering above the clouds . . . while southward, in the distance, is the majestic figure of Old Yonah."

If one takes a Geodetic Survey map and tries to take into consideration all these facts, it becomes *very* confusing. But, Track Rock is unlikely (1) it is not a spur of the Blue Ridge; (2) its elevation is very low and certainly not on a top; (3) Tray is not east from there, but southeast; (4) even in 1834 when men had good legs it's doubtful that one would walk there from Nacoochee Valley—definitely not by 6 a.m.; (5) the carvings—those that are left after the vandals—do not fit the description and the number.

I talked to a Mr. Elrod in Robertstown. He'd never heard of anything like Enchanted Mountain. His son, Hugh Elrod, a policeman in Cleveland, hadn't either, but he sent me to Mr. Charlie Winn in Choestoe Valley. No luck there either. Several mountains were mentioned with rocks or cliffs on them (Blood, Cowrock, Naked Mountain, and Steedy Mountain)—but not carvings that anyone knew. So, either the books are talking about Track Rock Gap in completely inaccurate terms, or else some exceptional carvings have been lost and forgotten.

If you have any information, I would certainly appreciate very much hearing from you. I am sending a copy of this letter to the Department of Archaeology at the University in Athens, in the hope that someone there has access to further references than my own library affords. Thank you very much for troubling to read all this. Perhaps we can help find a very mysterious mountain?

The Fragments of Chief Lacoonah
(With Apologies to Guy Davenport's "CARMINA ARCHILOCHI")

the only good
white man

is a dead
white man

                                                 wha(t) (ne)xt,
                                                 Red Necks?

they all
smell
a-
like

                                                     seen
                                                     one
                                                     seen
                                                     em
                                                     all

     xxxx

     ( )   (thoro)ugh(ly)
      my   (to)ugh
)((la)ugh(ter)
    (   )
      !

                Genuine Wh(ite) (Ma)n,
                be photographe(d) with
                (Gen)uine Cherokee
                (I)ndian

       ! ! ! ! ! ! ! ! ! ! ! !
             scalp

        (   )   Gr(eat) (Spir)it
                                             suggest
      itch!   Yellow Jacket
                                           Soup
                                              (?)
                                           Snake Pie,
                                         Corn (P)one (?)

whe(n)   Mullein Tea
visiting   pee (?)
a Sa(c)red Town
I always stay
at a
Holiday Inndian

The Laconic, Contrapuntal Nocturne of Two Goatsuckers,
Atop the Lean-To at Addis Gap,
Interrupted by a Disturbed Barn Owl*

chuck-will-widow chuck-will-widow
whip-poor-weel   *whip-poor-weel*
chuck-will-widow chuck-will-widow
whip-poor-weel   *whip-poor-weel*
chuck-will-widow chuck-will-widow
whip-poor-weel   *whip-poor-weel*

KSCHH! KSCHH! KSCHH! KSCHH! KSCHH! KSCHH! KSCHH! KSCHH!

chuck-will-widow chuck-will-widow
whip-poor-weel   *whip-poor-weel*
will   will
weel   *weel*
will   will
weel   *weel*
etc.   etc.
etc.   *etc.*

*owleatoric theory bets on two more interruptions
before the night is over

The Poet Sits Down to Make Jargonelles,
But First Scans the Beloved Objects to His Left, Center and Right:

1 Whitman, in a Matthew Brady photograph
2 "Stieglitz, Hart Crane, Stephen Crane, Dreiser, Marsden Hartley, Sherwood Anderson, and Dr. Williams," a drawing by James McGarrell for a future book by Edward Dahlberg
3 an etching of the East Anglia coast at Dunwich by Charles Keene
4 a blue watercolour by Henry Miller
5 a photograph by Aaron Siskind
6 an envelope from Charles Olson aired to Hampstead in 1963 with 15 one-cent stamps on it
7 "The Herdsman's Cottage," etching by Samuel Palmer
8 a ceramic alchemical-form by M. C. Richards
9 "Death by Water," a brass engraving by Stanley William Hayter
10 a plaster cast of Blake's life-mask by J. S. DeVille
11 aquatint of Gustav Mahler by Arthur Pavnzen
12 ink drawing of Anton Bruckner by Aubrey Schwartz
13 ink drawing of a Lakeland shepherd and sheep by Barry Hall
14 a miniature drawing of an Auerhahn by Philip Van Aver
15 vase of bittersweet

1 old oak desk
2 cold Olympia-Portable typewriter
3 pile of unpaid bills, the *Sierra Club's* on top
4 pile of correspondence, with a postcard from the Haags Gemeentemuseum of R. B. Kitaj's portrait of Norman Douglas, "The Master of Sentences," on top
5 Baby Ben saying 8:07 a.m.
6 pile of magazines, with October 1964 issue of *Liberation* on top
7 bottle of anti-appetite pills
8 heavily frosted window, the last drooping chrysanthemums, rhododendron hedge, and hemlock forest
9 Charles Ives, in a photograph by W. Eugene Smith

1 photograph of kids in haunted house by Ralph Eugene Meatyard
2 decorative plaster detail from a destroyed building in Chicago by Louis Sullivan
3 gouache by Dan Rice
4 drawing of a dove in flight by Emerson Woelffer
5 "Europa & the Bull," drawing by Reuben Nakian
6 "Great Pink, Blue-Eyed Bird," watercolour by Kenneth Patchen
7 "Visionary Portrait of Patchen," graphite drawing by Bruce Conner
8 weed photograph by Harry Callahan
9 "Yellow Clown," color aquatint by Rouault
10 untitled monoprint by Enid Foster
11 reading lamp
12 celibate couch

—all of which conspires to send the poet on a walk up the mountain and puts off a Jargonelle until the next page . . .

The Deracination

definition: *root*,

"a growing point,
an organ of absorption, an aereating organ,
a good reservoir, or
means of support"

Vernonia glauca, order *Compositae*,
"these tall perennials with
corymbose cymes of bright-purple heads of
tubular flowers
with conspicuous stigmas"

I do not know the Ironweed's root,
but I know it rules September

and where the flowers tower
in the wind there is a burr of
sound—empyrean . . . the mind
glows and the wind drifts . . .

epiphanies pull up
from roots—

epiphytic, making it up

out of the air

Osiris, From His Cave to Spring:

for the Scripture is written:
"Plants at One End, Birds at the Other!"

houseleek & garlic,
hyssop & mouse;

hawk & hepatica,
hyacinth, finch!

crawl, all
exits

from
hibernaculum!

"The best remedy for sore feet is Instant Jack Daniels (just add water). However, do not, I repeat *do not*, soak your feet in it. Drink it and let it work itself internally to the feet . . . I too have been hiking in the mountains, High Sierra, climbing Mount Dana and observing alpine flora and the Sierra Rosy Finch (found only above the tree-line feeding on insects fallen in the snow banks). Now back in the lowlands observing *Turdus migratorius*. When I see a robin and think of its names I get a Blakean vision of a long, gurgling sewer pipe with a dark shape moving leisurely down to the sea. And that, I think, is sufficient natural history for today."

Dave Haselwood

"So you have re-possessed the Hudson—surely not in the name of the Confederacy? It might interest you to know that an exploratory party, Sergeant Metcalf commanding, penetrated within the borders of Maine and accomplished a successful assault on South Turner Peak, commanding, as it does, a superlative view of Mount Katahdin, surrounding lakes, etc. . . . Have been reading some of your Ecology, Marston Bates in particular. Most interesting item so far: Athenian culture flourished immediately following destruction, at hand of man, of Mediterranean forests (memories of this in Homer, ancient Sicilian forests, forest fires, etc.)—situation comparable to ours today: the remembered and almost-remembered and vanished wilderness. Well to remember that ours is the *only* lively contemporary culture in the world today, god help us all. This fits in neatly with the psychologists, bless 'em, the notion of art as corrective measure, attempt to compensate, etc.—we feel somehow raped, are trying to grow back what has been taken. Am happy to concur with this."

Paul Metcalf

"Your Appalachian journal sounds delicious, and I look forward to tasting it, with a touch of sour cream to bring out the loganberry flavor . . . This is what keeps Troy in the news— I mean the Homer of it. Keep away from literary personages and pursuits—it makes the cream turn bad. Maybe that's what drove Whitman to his truck drivers and streetcar conductors? To keep fresh. Douglas too, searching always for the Unspoiled Mind—not just the body but the totality. His 'boys' weren't 'interesting people'—just human. That you have had to walk the backwoods of North America to find it again is a critique of us city-slickers. It's a sad condition when you have to find nature in the woods."

Walter Lowenfels

"The crucial, painful, only point is that one's land (mountains, trails, earth, nature) is connected to the society inhabiting that land in a way far different from what we imagine or from what our ancestors were used to. It is very possible that you have walked along a Trail that will be uninhabitable for the next 50 years if the Power that claims this land is the USA and continues on its own present path."

Gladney Oakley

The Whole Scene,
in a Two-Hundred-Year-Old
Demographic Nutshell

a long row to hoe—
too wet to plough

Blues & Roots/Rue & Bluets
is set in
Times New Roman
and printed by
The Meriden Gravure Company
on Fontana Suede paper

Book design and
typographic visualizations
of the
countrified concretions
by
Dana Atchley
1971